Sea Life
Follow-the-Dots

Barbara Soloff Levy

DOVER PUBLICATIONS, INC.
Mineola, New York

Bibliographical Note

Sea Life Follow-the-Dots is a new work, first published by Dover
Publications, Inc., in 1996.

International Standard Book Number

ISBN-13: 978-0-486-29446-9
ISBN-10: 0-486-29446-3

Manufactured in the United States by Courier Corporation
29446307
www.doverpublications.com

Publisher's Note

This book is full of life: sea life, that is. It contains 46 follow-the-dots pictures of all kinds of sea animals. Have fun learning while you complete pictures of fish, coral and other sea creatures. Read the caption to find out a little about each animal, then look at the solutions to find out what it is called. Using a pencil, simply draw a line from dot 1, to dot 2, to dot 3, and so on, until the picture is complete. After you're done with a picture, you might want to color it in. Well, go right ahead! Enjoy!

Sea Life
Follow-the-Dots

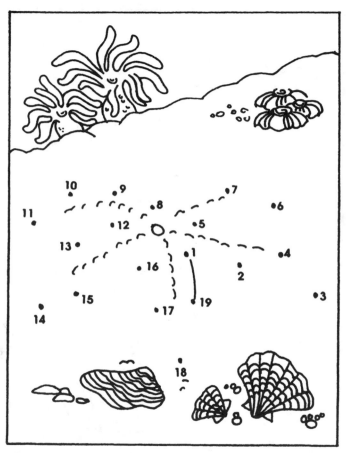

This star-shaped creature can often be found washed up on the beach. Go ahead, pick it up!

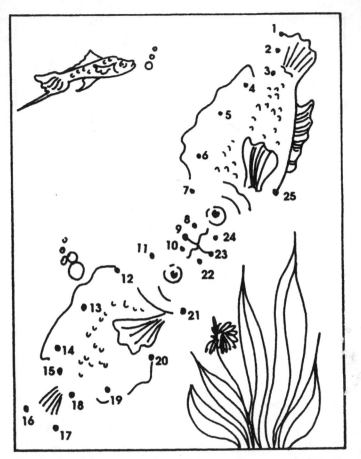

These popular aquarium fish are famous for their peculiar humanlike activities.

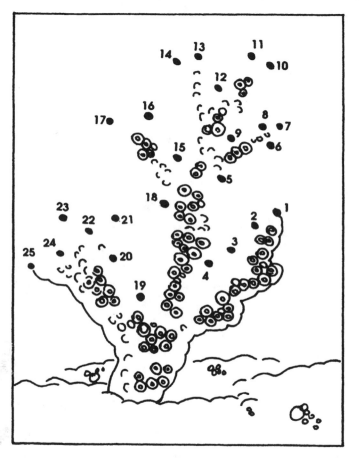

The delicate branches of this colony of creatures spread out like animal horns.

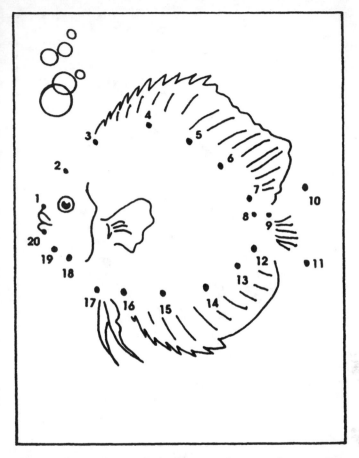

These astonishing fish are nearly round, very flat and come in a myriad colors.

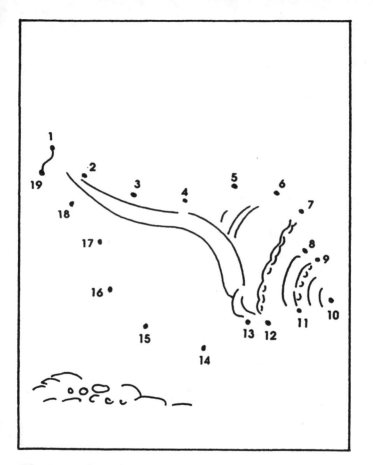

They say that if you put this shell up to your ear you can hear the ocean, no matter where you are!

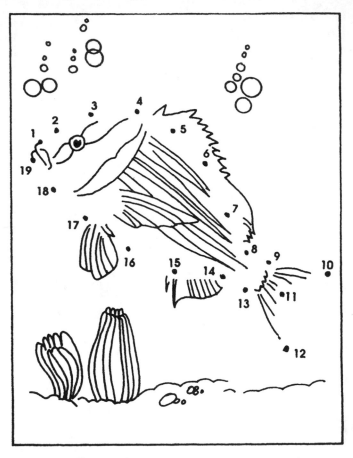

The bumblebee of the sea? This fish is marked by black and yellow stripes.

14

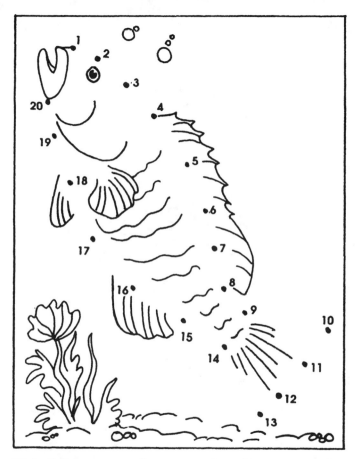

This fish has a very large mouth and can grow to be eight feet long.

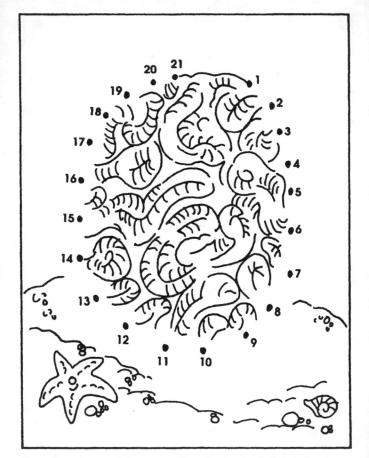

It may live in the sea, but it looks like a human brain!

16

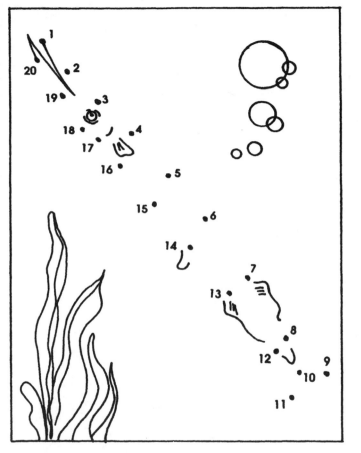

This species of fish is 220 million years old and has a mouth like an alligator's.

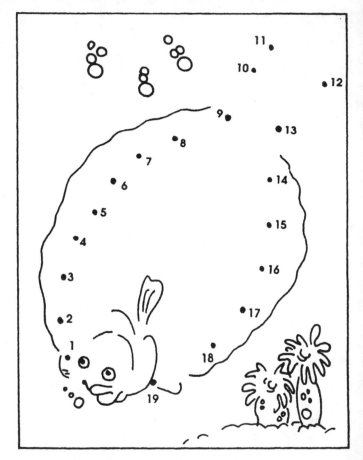

These flat fish live on the sandy ocean floor and have both eyes on one side of their head.

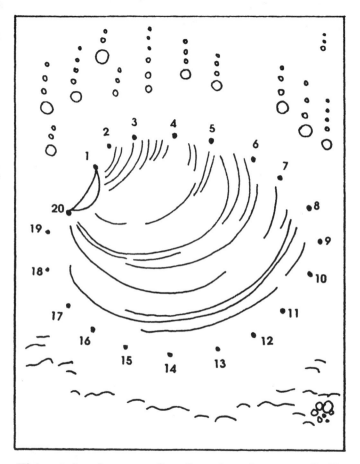

This animal moves by flapping its two shells together.

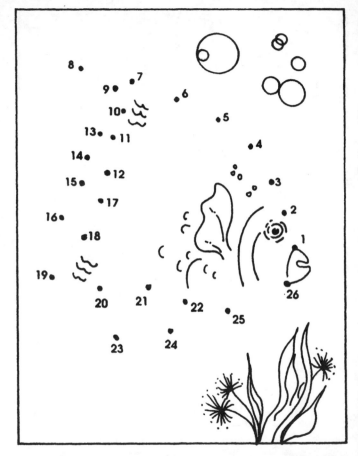

A colorful, triangular fish, it has large fins that look like angel's wings.

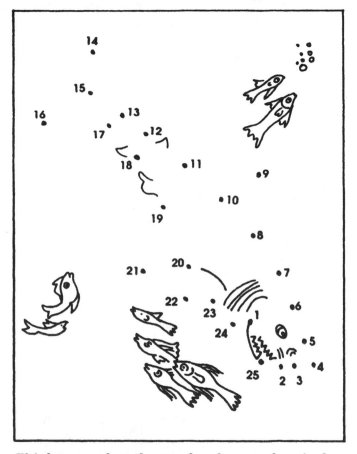

This huge predator has teeth as long as three inches and has been the subject of several movies. Can you guess it?

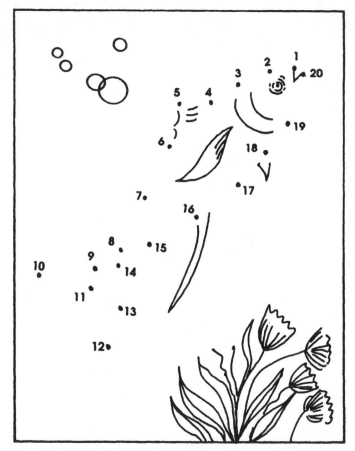

Sometimes called the "chicken of the sea," it has a yellow stripe on its side and fins.

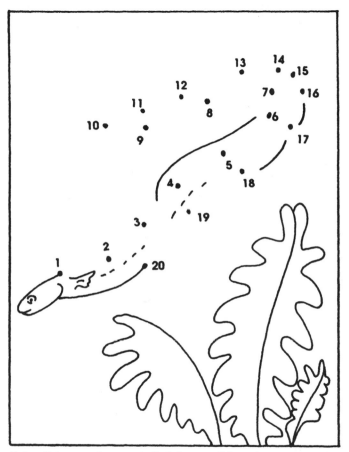

It's slippery, long and thin, and it migrates up to 2000 miles each year to reproduce!

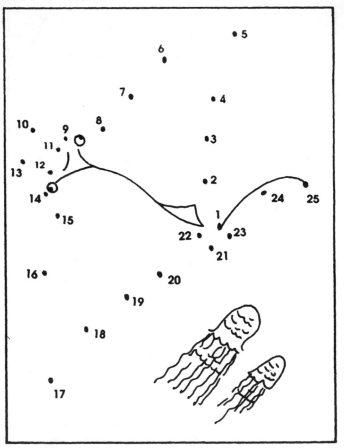

This extraordinary animal appears to be flying as it moves gracefully through the water.

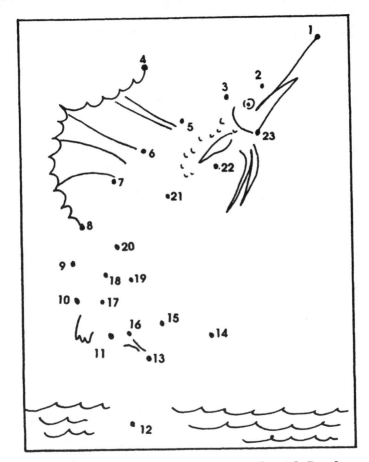

This large ocean fish has a high dorsal fin that looks like a sail.

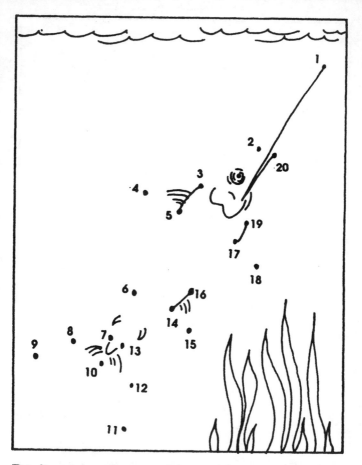

Don't get too close to this one! Its sharp nose is shaped like a sword.

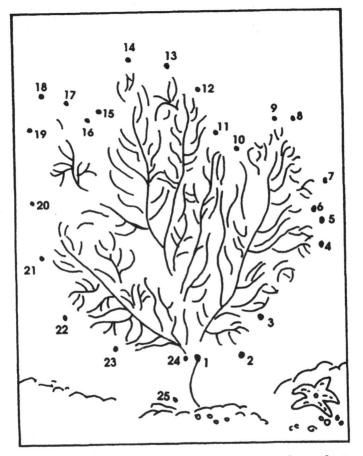

These creatures join together to form a colony that
fans out and sways in the motion of the waves.

Some species of this short, stout fish have long horns on their foreheads, like bulls!

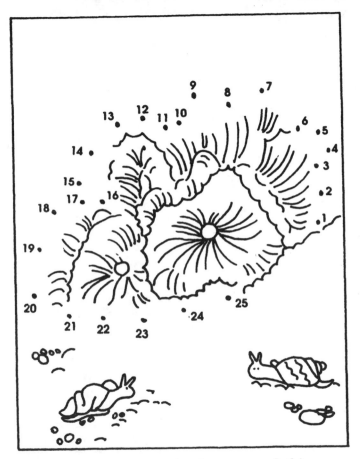

There are many colors in the sea, and this rose-colored creature adds to the beauty of the underwater world.

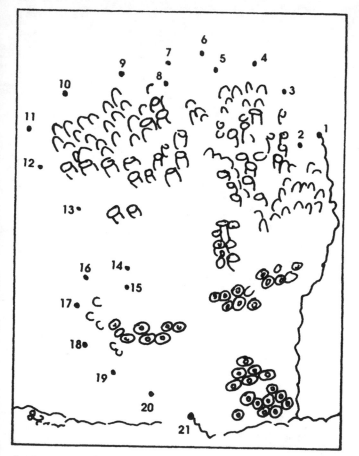

As it grows, this coral resembles the antlers of some land animals.

This organism stings approaching predators for protection.

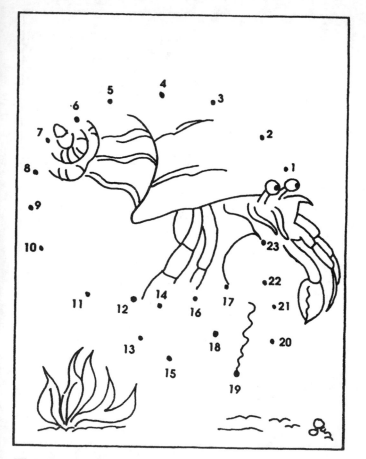

This funny animal lives in the discarded shells of other creatures, often snails.

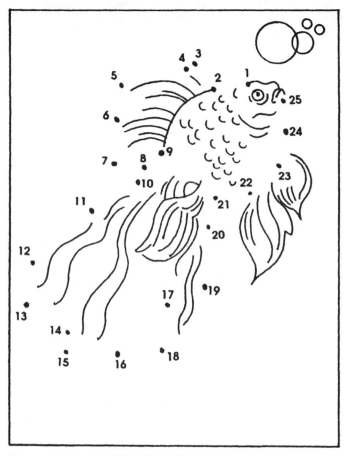

Do you have a fish bowl? You may have some of these.

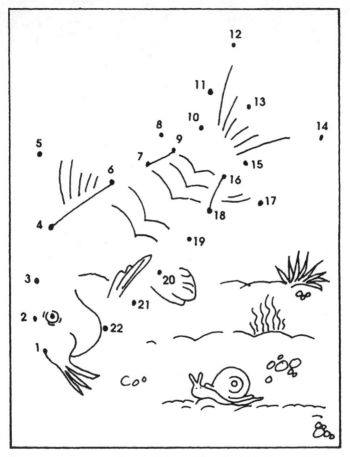

It doesn't purr, but it has long whiskers like a friendly feline.

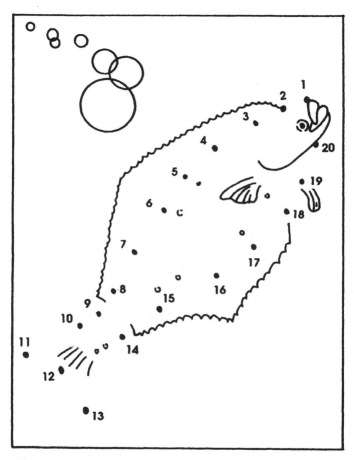

This flat fish changes color to match the color of the ocean floor.

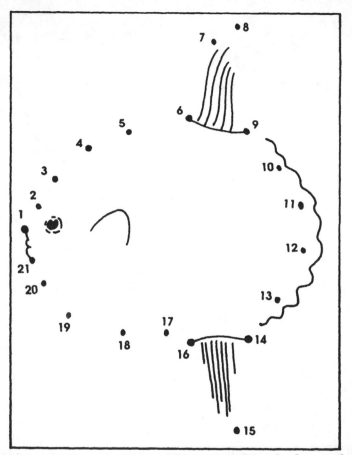

Its head is as big as the rest of its body, and sometimes it floats just below the surface of the water.

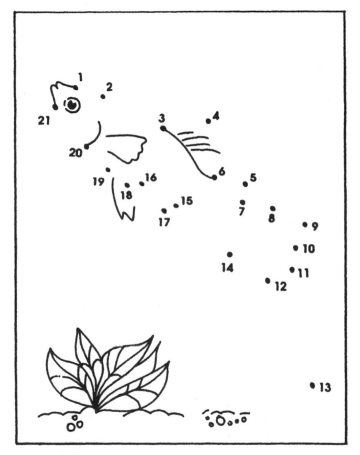

This tiny aquarium fish has a long swordlike tail and beautiful olive and yellow markings.

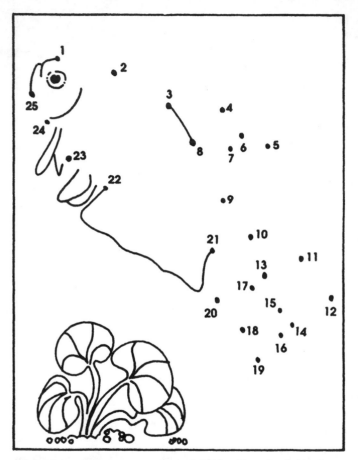

Colors, colors everywhere! This South American fish comes in every color of the rainbow, and more!

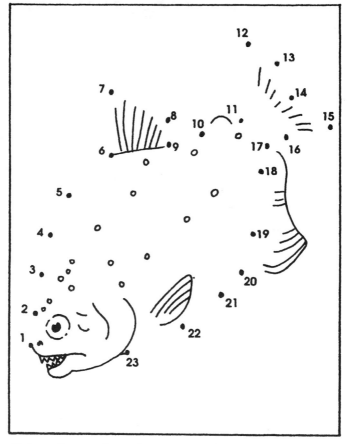

Tales of horror have been created about the ferocious teeth and powerful jaws of these voracious, terrifying fish.

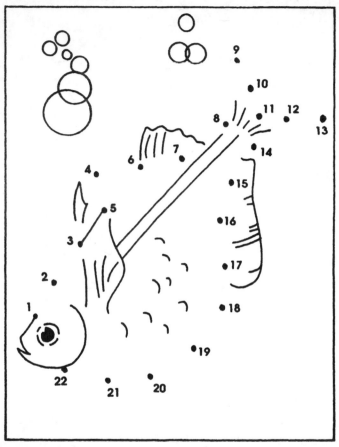

These two-inch-long fish have a big, round belly, live in the deep sea, and eat plankton for breakfast, lunch and dinner.

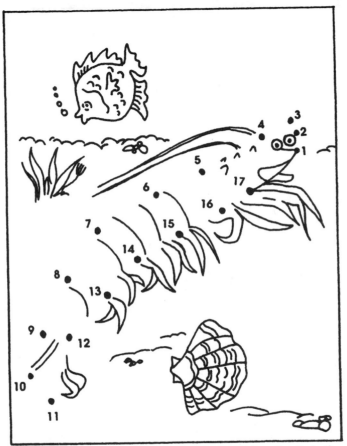

This small crustacean is harvested for food daily around the world.

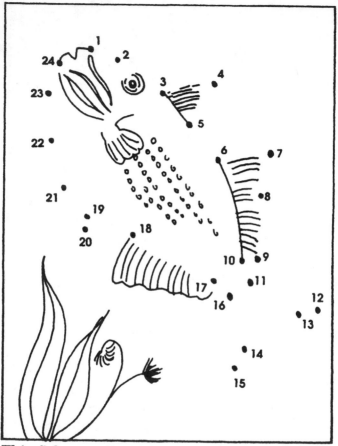

This fish uses a wild array of colors, stripes and patches as camouflage. Color it in!

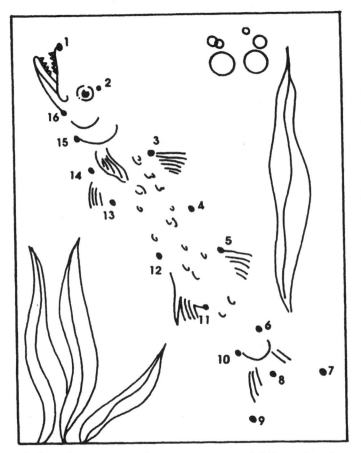

It can grow up to eight feet long, and divers fear its excellent predatory skills.

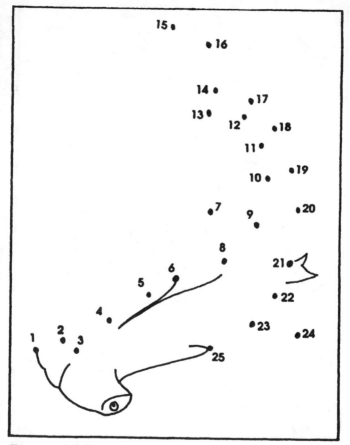

Do you think you could use the head of this strange fish to do a little carpentry? It might not like that very much.

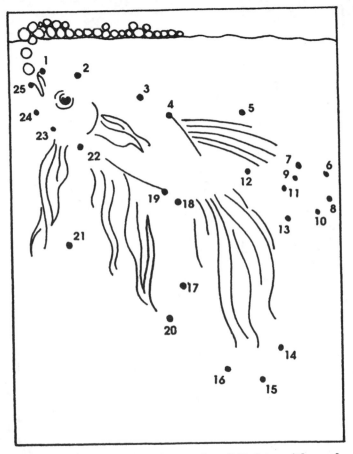

These minuscule fish have ritual fights with each other than can last 15 minutes or longer!

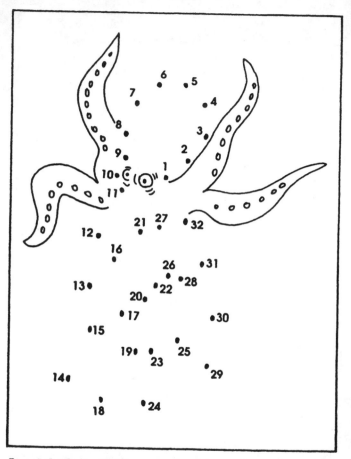

Its eight long limbs armed with suction cups make this one of the oddest creatures in the sea.

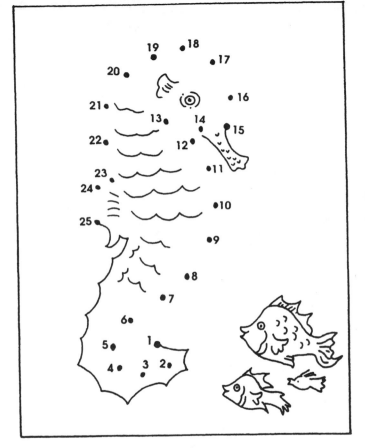

It has a horse's head but it lives underwater. What is it?

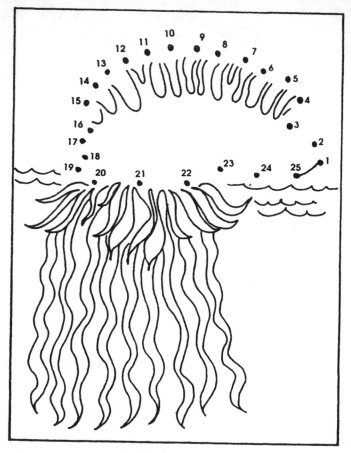

The sting of this huge jellyfish can kill a large fish.

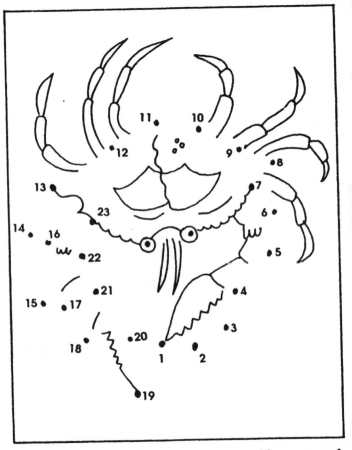

This bottom-dwelling creature runs sideways and
burrows under ground when attacked.

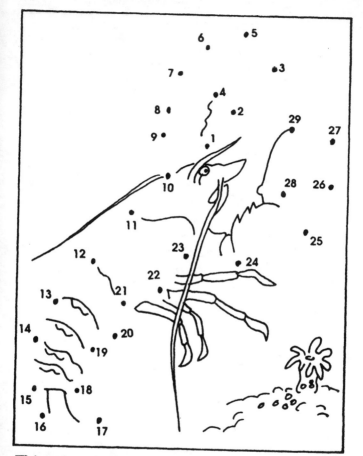

This spiny crustacean lives for 100 years, or longer!

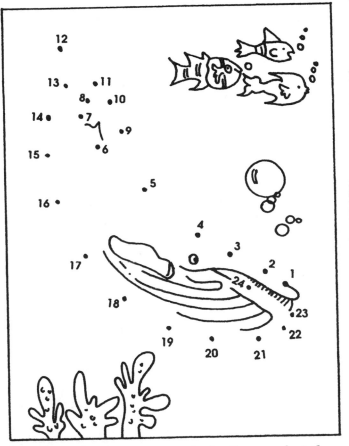

They are the largest animals in the sea, but they aren't fish! Do you know what they are?

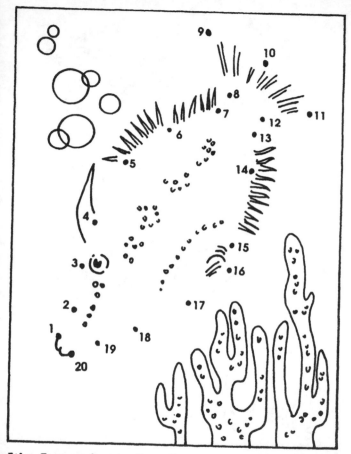

It's flat and round and can disguise itself by changing colors rapidly.

52

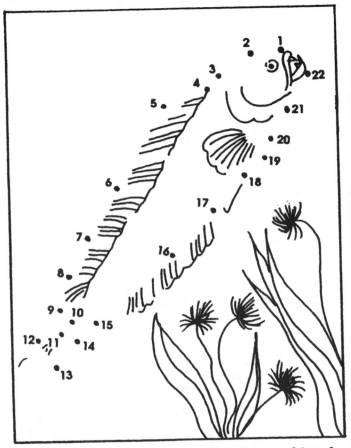

Its gray skin and aggressive nature caused it to be
named after a fearsome land animal.

This fast fish can swim up to 37 miles per hour, but don't mistake it for the mammal with a similar name.

Solutions

Solutions